M000081588

The Little
Book of
Happiness

The Little
Book of
Happiness

Miriam Akhtar MAPP

An Hachette UK Company
www.hachette.co.uk

First published in Great Britain in 2019 by Gaia,
an imprint of Octopus Publishing Group Ltd
Carmelite House
50 Victoria Embankment
London EC4Y 0DZ
www.octopusbooks.co.uk

Distributed in the US by Hachette Book Group
1290 Avenue of the Americas, 4th and 5th Floors,
New York, NY 10104

Distributed in Canada by Canadian Manda Group
664 Annette St., Toronto, Ontario, Canada M6S 2C8

ISBN 978-1-85675-400-2

A CIP catalogue record for this book is available from the British Library.

Printed and bound in China.

10 9 8 7 6 5 4 3 2 1

Commissioning Editor: Leanne Bryan
Senior Editor: Pollyanna Poulter
Copy Editor: Mandy Greenfield
Art Director: Juliette Norsworthy
Designer and Illustrator: Abi Read
Production Controller: Emily Noto

Contents

Introduction

Ask someone what they most wish for in their life and the likely response is that they want to be happy. Happiness is a major goal for humans and a subject that has fascinated thinkers and teachers for millennia.

It could be the feeling of joy when you're out having fun or a moment of serenity during a meditation. Happiness is there in the connection with someone you love, and comes from the satisfaction of living your life with purpose or in the simple contentment that life is exactly the way it was meant to be.

People naturally want to feel good, but can you *make* yourself happy or is it something that happens accidentally when you're busy making other plans? The paradox of happiness is that the more you chase it, the more elusive it can seem.

In Buddhism the pursuit of happiness is seen as the root cause of *unhappiness*, creating a craving and dissatisfaction with life. And modern science agrees with ancient spiritual wisdom. People who value happiness highly often set standards for it that are hard to obtain, leading them to feel disappointed and lowering their happiness, the more they want it. So how can we build sustainable wellbeing without falling into this trap?

The good news is that there is now a science to happiness, investigating questions such as what makes us happy, what gives meaning to life and how we flourish. Known as "positive psychology", it has been around since the turn of the 21st century and has produced a body of evidence on what it takes to increase our happiness. Positive psychology interventions are "treatment methods or intentional activities that aim to cultivate positive feelings, behaviours or cognitions", according to a study by Nancy Sin and Sonja Lyubomirsky, and a number of studies have shown how they significantly enhance wellbeing and ameliorate depressive symptoms. This book is grounded in that research, and each of the 12 Happiness Habits (see page 40) is backed by science.

1. What is Happiness?

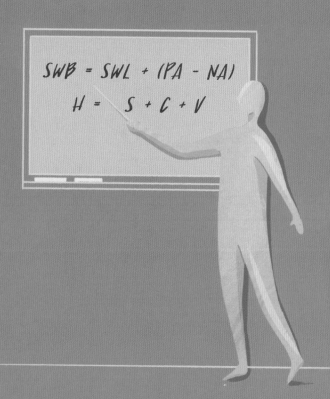

$$SWB = SWL + (PA - NA)$$
$$H = S + C + V$$

Two Kinds of Happiness

There are two major dimensions to the science of happiness, both of which originated with the ancient Greek philosophers:

Hedonic wellbeing (the clue is in the name!) comes from "hedonism" and is about the pursuit of pleasure. It's the feel-good factor, with all the fun and frolics. The focus, in hedonic wellbeing, is on maximizing pleasure and minimizing pain. It's the better-known form of happiness that is experienced in those peak moments of enjoyment.

Eudaimonic wellbeing is the umbrella term for a deeper kind of contentment, which comes from a sense of meaning, personal growth and self-actualization. The Greek philosopher Aristotle's original concept of *eudaimonia* was about leading a life of virtue, and the modern take is akin to functioning well and flourishing. In practice, eudaimonic wellbeing is about having a sense of purpose, using your strengths, doing something good in the world, experiencing "flow" (see page 18), positive relationships, autonomy and a feeling of competence and confidence in yourself. It may be a multifaceted idea, but it can be summed up in a simple formula: eudaimonic wellbeing comes from putting effort into something that is meaningful to you that goes beyond the self.

Effort + Meaning =
Eudaimonic Wellbeing

Money and happiness

Does money make you happy? The relationship between money and happiness is...complicated, to say the least. Being unable to afford the necessities of life will certainly make you unhappy, but once those needs are covered, a higher income doesn't correlate with equally high levels of happiness. Plus there's the added stress of managing your wealth to consider.

How you spend your time counts. People who prioritize wealth tend to be less happy than those who put their relationships first. What you spend your money on is also a factor. Using money for experiences – ideally shared ones – has a greater return on your wellbeing than buying material goods. So focus on relationships rather than retail to maximize your happiness.

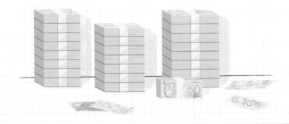

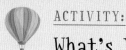

ACTIVITY:

What's Your Balance?

Happiness is about getting the balance right for *you* between the pursuit of pleasure (hedonic wellbeing) and having a sense of purpose (eudaimonic wellbeing).

Take a look at the chart opposite and see if you can identify which box you are in right now. Which box would you *like* to be in? What small steps could you take to get there?

There's no right or wrong answer here as to what will work best for you. Maybe you've been partying hard and it's time to get serious about your work. Or you're studying and working hard and some pure pleasure could be just the tonic you need.

You *can* have too much of a good thing, though. Overdoing the sweet life can become indulgent, leaving you sluggish, unmotivated and dissatisfied; meanwhile, too much of the dry life can leave you feeling pressurized, unable to enjoy yourself and with your relationships under strain.

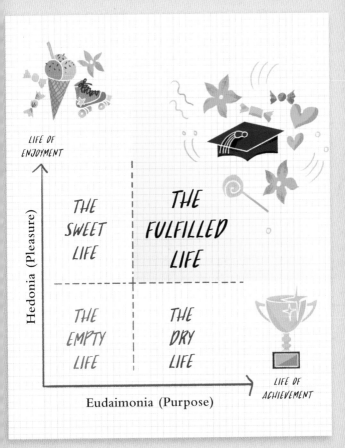

LIFE OF
ENJOYMENT

Hedonia (Pleasure)

THE
SWEET
LIFE

THE
FULFILLED
LIFE

THE
EMPTY
LIFE

THE
DRY
LIFE

LIFE OF
ACHIEVEMENT

Eudaimonia (Purpose)

The Science of Happiness

"Happiness" and "wellbeing" are words that are used interchangeably in positive psychology, but the official term is "Subjective Wellbeing" (SWB), which is based on how we evaluate our life.

As a science, it naturally comes with its own formulae, such as the one below, which is used to measure subjective wellbeing.

$$SWB = SWL + (PA - NA)$$

🐓 **Satisfaction With Life (SWL)** is the way you rate your life. Are you making progress toward your goals? Or is there a gap between where you are now and where you'd like to be? How satisfied are you with various areas of life, such as work or home? This is the cognitive side of happiness – how you judge your life.

🐓 **Positive Affect (PA)** is the sum of your experience of positive emotions and its ratio to **Negative Affect (NA)**. What is your balance of positive to negative emotions like? Do you experience more positive than negative emotions, or vice versa? This is the emotional side of happiness – how you feel.

Professor Martin Seligman, the co-founder of positive psychology, gives the following formula in his classic book, *Authentic Happiness*.

$$H = S + C + V$$

🐔 **H** refers to your **Happiness** baseline.

🐔 The **Set Range (S)** is your genetic setpoint for happiness, inherited from your biological family. Your level of happiness will fluctuate in response to major life events, but tends to revert to its normal range.

🐔 Your **Circumstances (C)** – such as what you do for work or where you live – are often what you look to change when you want to grow your happiness, and yet these factors have a relatively minor influence on your wellbeing.

🐔 The **Voluntary (V)** part is your window of opportunity. This is about your choice of mindset and the practices you engage in. Developing the 12 Happiness Habits (see page 40) will help you make the most of this element, which lies under your direct influence.

Authentic Happiness to PERMAnent Wellbeing

Professor Martin Seligman's original theory of authentic happiness had three pathways to it: the pleasant life (P), the engaged life (E) and the meaningful life (M). He went on to expand this into the PERMA model of wellbeing, introducing an R and A in his 2011 book *Flourish*. This was to acknowledge that happiness is more than just feeling good; positive psychology is more than a "happyology" – it is the science of wellbeing.

All these elements make a contribution to your wellbeing. If you can put a tick against them, you are on course to flourish: a state of high wellbeing.

Positive emotion is about enjoyment (see page 25) and was previously known as the pleasant life.

Engagement is a state of absorption known as "flow" (see page 18).

Relationships are about our need for social connectedness (see page 67).

ENGAGED LIFE

ASANT LIFE

MEANINGFUL LIFE

🐦 **Meaning** is having a purpose that goes beyond the self (see page 56).

🐦 **Accomplishment** means making progress and achieving success (see page 91).

Getting physical

Wellbeing is holistic and includes what is going on below the head, so suggestions have been made to expand the PERMA framework to include the physical dimension. The PERMAH model has an H for Health, to represent eating well, physical activity and quality sleep, while PERMA-V adds V for Vitality.

Finding Your Flow

Ever been so absorbed in what you're doing that hours seem to fly by without you noticing? This is "flow", a deeply satisfying state of total immersion.

Many creative pastimes can get you into flow. The repetitive movement of knitting, for example, stimulates the release of serotonin, which is one of the happy hormones. Flow is an optimal experience, which Professor Mihaly Csikszentmihalyi, the joint co-founder of positive psychology, contributed to the field.

How you know you're in flow

🐔 You are completely absorbed.

🐔 You feel at one with what you're doing.

🐔 You lose track of time.

🐔 You lack self-consciousness.

🐔 What you're doing is intrinsically rewarding.

To enter into a state of flow, you need to find the sweet spot between the level of challenge in the activity you're undertaking and your capacity in the area. High challenge matched by high skill is the perfect combination to go into flow. If there is too little challenge relative to your skill, you may get bored, whereas too much challenge could trip you into anxiety.

Once you find your flow, it's a very satisfying experience, although this is generally something that you notice *after* the event. While you are in it, flow is completely emotionless.

What pulls you into flow?

- A balance of challenge and skill.
- A simple and compelling goal.
- Clear feedback: you know exactly how you're doing.

2. The Benefits of Happiness

Happiness is Good For You

It's official. Happiness doesn't just feel good,
it does you good, too. It can even help you live
longer. A key piece of evidence comes from the
Nun Study, a longitudinal study of the School
Sisters of Notre Dame in the USA.

The sisters wrote autobiographical essays and, decades
later, their content was analysed for the presence of positive
emotions and then compared with mortality rates. The sisters
lead very similar lives, in terms of diet and daily routine,
making it easier to assess the impact of subjective wellbeing
on their longevity. By the age of 85, 79 percent of the most
cheerful nuns were still alive, compared to 54 percent of the
least cheerful. By age 93, only 18 percent of the least cheerful
were alive, compared to just over half (52 percent) of the
happiest nuns.

Happy people function better and experience other advantages:

🐦 Stronger immune systems

🐦 Greater optimism

🐦 More creativity

🐦 Better ability to multitask, stay on task and be systematic

- Greater sociability and popularity among friends and colleagues
- Higher levels of trust and helpfulness
- Less hostility and self-centredness
- Higher income levels.

Happiness and success

Yes, it turns out that happiness is good for the bank balance. There is a virtuous relationship between happiness and success. It's natural to feel good when something goes well, but the reverse is equally true. People who have high levels of wellbeing are more likely to enjoy success across multiple domains of life, ranging from marriage and friendship to health and performance at work. This is why it's worth focusing on your wellbeing, not only for your personal happiness, but also for your professional success.

The Joy of Positive Emotions

Awe, bliss, calm, delight, excitement – who doesn't love a positive emotion? But is there anything more to these good feelings than a pleasant, uplifting experience?

Professor Barbara Fredrickson, who leads the Positive Emotions and Psychophysiology Lab at the University of North Carolina, has spent her career investigating this. Her Broaden-and-Build Theory of Positive Emotions explains exactly why positivity is good for us. Let's take a look at three ways that positive emotions help us. They:

Broaden our thought–action repertoires. Positive emotions open our minds up, broadening our capacity to see the bigger picture, to think flexibly and creatively and to act proactively. I had a lightbulb moment when I first heard this, because when I worked in the broadcast media I thought that being creative meant putting myself under maximum pressure, mainlining caffeine and pulling all-nighters. But now I do something fun, such as putting on a disco track and bouncing on my mini-trampoline, before diving into a spot of writing.

Build our inner resources. Although they are short-lived, positive emotions accumulate to form four types of resource that you can draw on whenever you need them:

1 **Psychological resources**, such as resilience and optimism, having a clear sense of who you are and what your goals are.

2 **Intellectual resources** to help you learn and solve problems.

3 **Social resources**, so that you're open to forming new connections and deepening existing bonds.

4 **Physical resources**, such as muscle strength, cardiovascular health and coordination. If you're wondering how positive emotions strengthen the body, think of how children respond when they're playing: having fun at the playground means moving the body and developing those junior muscles.

🌱 **Help us to bounce back from negativity.** Fredrickson calls this your "inner reset button". Positive emotions "undo" the effects of stress on the body, calming the heart and lowering blood pressure. The next time you have a stressful experience, try doing something that makes you smile and notice how it helps you recover your composure.

3. The Barriers to Happiness

Happiness Interrupted

If we had completely cracked the happiness code, we'd all be walking around with PERMA(nent) smiles – but that's not the case. As humans, we find it notoriously difficult to predict how events in the future will make us feel, and there are several obstacles that get in the way of our happiness.

Hedonic adaptation

This is the "taking it for granted" phenomenon, also known as the hedonic treadmill, where we get used to the source of happiness, so that the novelty starts to wear off. The second time you go to that top-rated restaurant is not quite as memorable as your first meal there. Those gorgeous clothes that looked so good in the shop lose their allure when they've been hanging in your wardrobe for a while. The solution is to add variety or to up the dose. This is one of the limitations of hedonic wellbeing (see page 9); if you want to sustain your happiness, you're better off choosing a route to eudaimonic wellbeing (see page 10), which has no such restrictions.

The Negativity Bias

The brain is wired to notice what's wrong before we notice what's right. Bad is stronger than good, and the psychological effects of bad things outweigh those of positive experiences.

This negativity bias is part of our survival mechanism and would have come in very handy when we were hunter-gatherers needing to avoid nasty threats such as sabre-toothed tigers. Unfortunately, this bias also operates when we're nowhere near danger. We'll notice the bored, restless man sitting in the audience before we see the others who are listening intently. Our eyes are drawn to the dirty windows before we see the fabulous interior design. What this means is that we need to work a little harder to overcome the negativity bias in order to cultivate positive emotions that will keep us on the path to happiness.

Positive vs negative

The nature of positive emotions is that they are fleeting, light experiences – a moment of joy or calm. Negative emotions, on the other hand, are big beasts that hang around; we speak about being "in the grip of fear", "consumed by anger" and "weighed down with sadness". The purpose of negative emotions is to keep us safe: they alert us to danger and let us know when something needs our urgent attention.

The Tyranny of Choice

Ten kinds of coffee to choose from, or 20 types
of peanut butter in the shop – the 21st century
offers so many choices that making a decision
can send you into overwhelm mode.

This "tyranny of choice" impacts happiness as it causes
anxiety and lowers wellbeing. People who get caught up
in the stress of this are known as "maximizers", according
to the American psychologist Professor Barry Schwartz.
Maximizers want the best and like to take their time to
weigh up a wide range of options, but often experience
regret or blame themselves when their choice fails to live up
to their expectations. They get the best bargains and highest

salaries, but it comes at a cost, because they suffer from perfectionism and upward social comparisons.

The antidote is to behave like a "satisficer" (the word combines "satisfy" and "suffice"), who goes for what's good enough, settling for the first option that meets their minimum criteria. I know a professor of psychology whose own quality of life improved the moment he traded being a maximizer for being a satisficer.

The comparison trap

We have a natural tendency to compare ourselves to others, although usually it's to people who we consider to be better off than we are, which can leave us feeling inadequate. This is exacerbated by social media, which offers endless possibilities of perfect-looking lifestyles that make us feel bad. It's not easy turning off these comparisons, but one way is to try to compare yourself with people who are worse off than you, rather than better. Compare down rather than up.

4. Happiness is a Practice

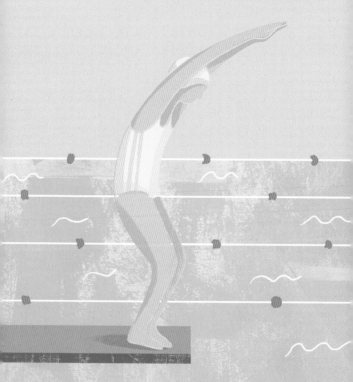

Diving into Happiness

Happiness is something we do, rather than something that just happens. Neuroscience has shown that the brain is malleable – not only being shaped by the events that happen to us, but also capable of being influenced by training.

In my coaching practice I find that people are often interested in the science of happiness, but sometimes miss the key point, which is that you have to go beyond intellectual curiosity and put the knowledge into practice in order to make a difference to your wellbeing.

To make a habit out of happiness requires repetition of behaviour to create new neural connections. Habits are behaviours that have become automatic; the brain likes these because they use low levels of energy. It takes anything from around three weeks to two months of significant repeats to form a new positive habit, which is easier to do than reforming an old bad habit. Once you have successfully automated a practice, you are more likely to continue it and reap the benefits of greater wellbeing. As your confidence grows by cementing one habit, you will feel more inclined to add other positive behaviours into your life.

Feeding Your Positivity

My top tip is to do the activities in this book regularly, but to relax and let go of the results. Sometimes they will work, sometimes they won't; but the more frequently you do them, the more often you will connect with an authentic positivity.

It is in the nature of positive emotions that you can't hang on to them. They are like butterflies – here one moment and gone the next; and contrary to expectations, it is not a good idea to "fake it until you make it". Feigning positivity can do more harm than good. It puts the hearts of cardiac patients under pressure, as do fake smiles that don't quite reach the orbicularis-oculi muscles around the eyes. These "non-enjoyment smiles" are known as "Pan Am smiles" – so-called after those of the flight attendants of the Jet Age.

It is the authentic, heartfelt experience of positive emotions that holds benefit. As you experience more regular positive emotions, you'll find yourself entering an upward spiral where the positivity builds, putting you on the path to flourishing and, ultimately, transforming both you and your life.

The top ten positive emotions

Positivity is the frequent experience of positive emotions. According to Barbara Fredrickson's research (see page 25), the top ten most frequently experienced positive emotions are:

- joy
- gratitude
- serenity
- interest
- hope
- pride
- inspiration
- amusement
- awe
- love

Putting love at the bottom of the list is a bit of a cheat as this is, in fact, our supreme positive emotion and, depending on the context, can encompass any of the other top ten. Love is elicited by the presence of others.

The Growth Mindset

Mindsets are sets of beliefs that we hold about the way the world works, and they shape our mental landscapes. Professor Carol Dweck from Stanford University has identified two mindsets: the fixed mindset and the growth mindset.

Someone in a **fixed mindset** believes that we're born with certain abilities, which aren't open to much development. So you're born happy or not, smart or not, sporty or not. These people are less likely to try something new, for fear of not getting it right the first time.

Someone in a **growth mindset** believes that – with enough effort, motivation and concentration – you can become better at most things, and that includes developing your capacity for happiness. These people are more willing to experiment and learn from what happens. They don't mind getting it wrong and are flexible about trying out different ways of doing things.

You may have a fixed mindset about some areas of life (such as relationships) and a growth mindset about others (such as your work). The good news is that it is possible to move from one mindset to another.

Choose to operate in a growth mindset as you experiment with the 12 Happiness Habits (see page 40) and aim for progress rather than perfection.

How to develop a growth mindset

- Observe your own mindset; you can choose to adopt a "growth mindset".

- Simply knowing about the growth mindset helps to develop one.

- When you face challenges, remind yourself about the growth mindset.

- Note the power of the word "yet": *"I've not mastered this…yet"*.

- Praise your efforts rather than the end result, to keep up your motivation.

Happiness is a Practice

5. The 12 Happiness Habits

Making a Habit of Happiness

The 12 Happiness Habits in this chapter are all evidence-based practices, so we know they work. Use them in whatever way appeals to you; the most important thing is to put the knowledge into practice. You could let your intuition guide you or be more systematic and tackle one habit a week, so that in three months you'll have mastered them all. Or make it a year in which to transform your life, by beginning each month with a new habit. Enjoy!

1 Learn to play

2 Express gratitude

3 Savour the positive

4 Harness your strengths

5 Live with meaning

6 Learn optimism

7 Value relationships

8 Practise kindness

9 Get physical

10 Turn to nature

11 Practise mindfulness

12 Strive for success

1. Learn to Play

A famous advertising slogan once enticed us to "work, rest and play", but while children need no encouragement to play, as adults we don't seem to have the space or the inclination for the fun factor.

Leisure activities are great ways to relax, take a break from everyday stresses, explore the world and learn something new. Playtime recharges the batteries so that we perform better at work, and the shared enjoyment nurtures relationships.

Play your way to happiness

🐓 Active recreation (such as sports, gardening, baking or dancing) has far more benefits for our wellbeing than passive leisure, such as watching TV.

🐓 Spending time on a hobby can take you into the satisfying state of "flow" (see page 18).

🐓 Professor Neil Frude, the psychologist who founded the "Books on Prescription" scheme (whereby patients with depression and anxiety are prescribed the healing benefits of self-help books), recommends a simple happiness formula of having: a) something to do, b) something to love and c) something to look forward to. He suggests writing a TFL list of **T**hings to **L**ook **F**orward to.

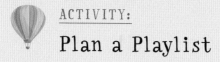

ACTIVITY:

Plan a Playlist

Just as you might have a playlist of your favourite tracks on your phone, you can do the same with leisure activities.

An idea inspired by *Quality of Life Therapy,* by Professor Michael Frisch, is to put together a playlist of active recreational pursuits and then schedule something from it every day. One of the benefits of having the list ready is that, when your mood sinks, you have a personal prescription for something that puts sunshine into your soul.

1 Write a list of ten recreational activities that you enjoy doing, such as singing in a choir, going to art exhibitions, crafting, quizzes, stand-up comedy or team sports.

2 Schedule something from your playlist every day, even if it's only for five or ten minutes.

3 Keep your playlist handy (put it in your diary or add it to your screensaver) to act as a reminder whenever you need a boost.

2. Express Gratitude

"Count your blessings" are the wise words that span faith and folklore. Now there is a body of research that confirms that adopting an attitude of gratitude has multiple benefits for wellbeing.

It develops our capacity for happiness and generates positivity, life satisfaction, optimism, hope, enthusiasm, energy, spirituality and forgiveness.
And it can lower levels of stress hormones, depression, anxiety, loneliness, envy, neuroticism and materialism.

Gratitude journal

There is far more to gratitude
than simply saying "thank you".
It trains the mind to tune in and notice
the good things in life, which is a way of overcoming the
brain's negativity bias (see page 30), whereby your attention
is directed to what's wrong before noticing what's right.
Gratitude develops our awareness of being the beneficiary
of good things that originate outside ourselves.

A gratitude journal is a great way of recalling all the good
stuff that happens, which you might otherwise forget.

Sonja Lyubomirsky, author of *The How of Happiness*,
recommends journalling at a frequency that feels right
for you. I go for once a week on a Sunday, so I can reflect
on the past week and prepare for the upcoming one.

I've kept gratitude journals now for more than 20 years
and it's the practice that has made the biggest difference,
changing my mindset from one of scarcity to one of
abundance. This is one of the first habits I teach.

ACTIVITY:

Three Good Things

Every day, make a list of three good things in your life: a positive event, such as getting good feedback on a piece of work; or a constant positive, such as enjoying good health or having a roof over your head. Use the following questions as prompts.

- What is good in your life?

- What are you grateful for? And who are you grateful to?

- What has gone well? And what was your role in making it happen?

You might find this hard at first, but you will soon start noticing things during the day that can go on your list.

Try anchoring three good things to a routine such as your commute, brushing your teeth or eating dinner. Making it something you do with family or friends is beneficial and helps it to become a habit.

3. Savour the Positive

While gratitude is about noticing the positives, savouring is about squeezing all the juice out of them to maximize the enjoyment.

Marvelling at the beauty of nature, feasting on a mouthwatering delicacy, cherishing the love of someone precious or treasuring a holiday memory – these are all examples of savouring. The process requires your full engagement. Think of it as being about the journey rather than the destination. Professors Fred Bryant and Joseph Veroff, the authors of *Savoring: A New Model of Positive Experience*, identify four key processes:

Thanksgiving: Reflection on the external world – gratitude for the good things in life.

Basking: Reflection on the internal world – pride in a job well done.

Marvelling: Absorption in the outer world (for instance, being awestruck by a magnificent view).

Luxuriating: Absorption in the internal world (such as the physical pleasure of a massage).

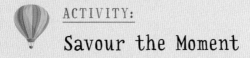

ACTIVITY:

Savour the Moment

Savouring is a process, rather than something that just happens. It's about bringing your attention to the small pleasures, so that you can make the most of them. These steps can help you engage with positive experiences when they occur.

1 Slow down and stretch out the experience.

2 Give the moment your full attention.

3 Apply your senses – sight, sound, smell, touch and taste.

4 Reflect on the source of enjoyment: *What do I appreciate here? What do I value?*

Once you've got the hang of savouring, you can apply it to anything at all – something concrete like the fragrance of a flower or something abstract like a happy memory.

Do be aware, though, that there is a subtle distinction between enhancing the experience and destroying it with too much focus.

4. Harness Your Strengths

Using your strengths helps you to feel good, function well and flourish. By harnessing your strengths you can boost your personal wellbeing, enhance your performance at work and strengthen your resilience, so that you're better able to get through the tough times.

There are two types of strength:

- **Character strengths** (also known as personal strengths): Positive qualities such as kindness or courage.

- **Performance strengths**: Abilities such as a talent for number-crunching or a gift for making people laugh.

Strengths vs weaknesses

Write down two lists: one of your strengths and one of your weaknesses. Which is longer? No surprise if it's the weaknesses, because people generally find it more challenging to name their strengths. Yet these are your assets, showing you at your best – the positive you. Your greatest potential for growth comes from developing your strengths rather than fixing your weaknesses.

Science of strengths

One of the early studies of positive psychology showed that finding new ways of using your strengths can lead to higher levels of happiness and lower levels of depression. Your strengths are your inner resources that protect your mental health and bring you energy, vitality, engagement, confidence, insight and perspective. If only we found it easy to identify our strengths…

ACTIVITY:

Discover Your Strengths

When you have a strength in play, you perform at your best, feel energized and look for more opportunities to use that strength. The questions below, drawn from Professor Alex Linley's *Average to A+*, can help you spot your strengths.

- What are you doing when you are at your best?

- What do you find easy and are naturally good at?

- When do you feel most alive? What energizes you?

- What sort of skill do you pick up effortlessly?

- What do you do just for the love of it?

- What are you passionate about?

- What makes you feel "This is the real me"?

- What were you good at as a child? How does it show up in your life now?

- What are you doing when you're "in flow" (see page 18)?

Take the VIA Survey

Another way of identifying your strengths is to take a test.
The VIA Survey is the result of a mammoth research task
to document humanity's positive characteristics. We all have
these universally valued strengths, in one order or another.
They are grouped together in six categories known as
"virtues" (see opposite).

You can take the VIA Inventory of Strengths test for free
by registering at www.viacharacter.org. Once you know
your own character strengths, they can turn into virtues,
if you invest in developing them.

Your strengths can be leveraged to help you reach your
goals and resolve issues. If you're at a crossroads in life,
such as maternity leave, retirement or redundancy, and
are unsure how to go forward, your strengths will give
you a clue as to which areas you'll succeed in, because
you're harnessing what you are naturally good at.

THE 24 CHARACTER STRENGTHS:

VIRTUE OF WISDOM

Creativity
Curiosity
Judgement/critical thinking
Love of learning
Perspective

VIRTUE OF COURAGE

Bravery
Honesty
Perseverance
Zest

VIRTUE OF HUMANITY

Love
Kindness
Social intelligence

VIRTUE OF JUSTICE

Teamwork
Fairness
Leadership

VIRTUE OF TEMPERANCE

Forgiveness
Humility
Prudence
Self-regulation

VIRTUE OF TRANSCENDENCE

**Appreciation of
beauty and excellence**
Gratitude
Hope
Humour
Spirituality

5. Live with Meaning

What is your *ikigai*, or purpose in life? Your reason to get up in the morning? Meaning and purpose in life are essential ingredients for wellbeing.

An international study in 2014 by psychologists Shigehiro Oishi and Ed Diener found that it wasn't low levels of life satisfaction that predicted suicide rates, but low levels of meaning in life. Having a sense of meaning performs two major functions.

- It gives us an understanding of the "*why*" in life: why we do the things we do. This is our bedrock, which helps us be resilient in times of stress.

- Meaning also gives us a purpose; something to aim for. This is the corresponding "*how*": how we direct our efforts to live our sense of meaning.

Some of the top sources of meaning are:

- Relationships – family and friends
- Making a contribution to society
- Personal development, such as learning new skills
- Justice – standing up for a cause
- Achievement – working toward goals
- Creativity – expressing yourself as an artist or musician
- Spirituality/philosophy – exploring the deeper questions of life
- Health – improving or recovering your health
- Pleasure, such as travelling
- Leaving a legacy to the world, such as passing on knowledge.

Discovering a sense of purpose

We generally *find* purpose in positive events such as becoming a parent. We connect the event to a set of pre-existing beliefs, so there is a feeling of things turning out exactly as they were meant to. On the other hand, we *construct* meaning out of life's negative events, as part of making sense of adversity or to create something positive out of something negative. This is why many people start up charities after undergoing traumatic experiences, to make a meaningful difference to others who are going through something similar. I constructed my own sense of purpose out of depression. My purpose now is to put people on the path to happiness, which is still the reason I get up in the morning.

A major life event is often the trigger to a new purpose in life, but you can also discover a purpose by being proactive and learning from others.

Your sense of purpose can range from that of the next hour to your bigger sense of purpose, which changes over the course of a lifetime. Your earlier purpose may have been to gain qualifications; right now it might be about a particular vocation or caring for family; and in future it might be about your legacy, passing on knowledge or reconnecting with an old passion. A sense of meaning is just as important toward the end of life. The shorter the lifespan, the more the need for meaning grows, and we don't want to fritter away our remaining time on pointless activities. Having a sense of purpose can make us live longer and be healthier.

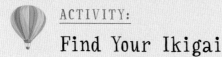

ACTIVITY:

Find Your Ikigai

Ikigai is a Japanese concept that means your reason for being, or the thing that gets you up in the morning. It is often described as having four overlapping elements, like a Venn diagram (see opposite). Where these converge is your *ikigai*.

The following questions can help you find your own *ikigai*.

🐓 What do you love? (your passion)

🐓 What does the world need? (your mission)

🐓 What are you good at? (your vocation)

🐓 What can you get paid for? (your profession)

Following your *ikigai* can give your life a rich source of meaning and open you up to eudaimonic wellbeing (see page 10).

WHAT YOU LOVE

PASSION

MISSION

WHAT YOU ARE
GOOD AT

IKIGAI

WHAT THE
WORLD NEEDS

VOCATION

PROFESSION

WHAT YOU CAN
BE PAID FOR

6. Learn Optimism

Optimism is known as the glue of the science of wellbeing, because everything positive sticks to it.

There are many advantages to thinking optimistically…

- Greater psychological and physical health

- Better quality of life

- More resilience and persistence

- Less distress when dealing with challenges

- Flexible coping strategies

- Better adaptation to negative events

…and just a couple of disadvantages.

- Optimists can underestimate risks, but pessimists tend to be more realistic.

- When disaster strikes, optimists may not be as well prepared as pessimists, but they are often better equipped to rebuild their lives subsequently.

Both optimism and pessimism act as self-fulfilling prophecies. If you have confidence in a positive outcome, you are more likely to put in the effort to guarantee success, whereas if you tend to be pessimistic, then you're more prone to giving up. This can turn into a downward spiral. Pessimism is a major risk factor for depression.

What if you're not a born optimist?

Optimism is a habit that you can develop, even if you lean naturally toward the half-empty glass. In *Learned Optimism*, Professor Martin Seligman describes a form of optimism known as optimistic explanatory or attributional style, based on how we explain to ourselves the causes and influences of previous events. This then affects the way that we think about the future.

The three Ps

There are three dimensions to optimistic and pessimistic thinking: the **Personal**, **Permanent** and **Pervasive**. When a negative event happens, optimists and pessimists think in opposite ways. Pessimists tend to think that the causes are internal (Personal), stable (Permanent) and global (Pervasive), whereas for optimists the causes are external (not personal), unstable (temporary) and local (limited to that circumstance).

Imagine a scenario where the company you work for has lost a catering contract. The table opposite shows how a pessimist's response will differ from that of an optimist.

When considering this example you can clearly see how, by thinking in the way they do, optimists are better able to protect themselves from strong, negative emotions.

Think positive

Think like an optimist when something goes wrong. How might the cause of the event be NOT personal, NOT permanent and NOT pervasive?

THREE P RESPONSES

PESSIMIST SAYS	OPTIMIST SAYS
Me (Personal)	**Not me (Not personal)**
It's all my fault. I'm no good at catering.	*Their business is in financial difficulty.*
Always (Permanent)	**Not always (Not permanent)**
It's always going to be like this.	*Last month we picked up a new client.*
Everywhere (Pervasive)	**Not everywhere (Not pervasive)**
The business is going down.	*There's a new market in pop-up restaurants.*

ACTIVITY:

Challenge the Three Ps

Next time a negative event happens in your life, try the following ways to challenge the three Ps of pessimism.

1 To contest the **Personal** dimension, look to the bigger picture and notice what other factors might have caused the negative event – whether it involves other people or circumstances.

2 To challenge the **Permanent** dimension, seek evidence that contradicts the belief that the situation is permanent. If that feels too difficult, look at how much of life *does* change – the year has its seasons, for instance.

3 To counter the **Pervasive** dimension, look at what areas of life *are* going well. For example, your professional life may well be in the doldrums, but you recognize that your relationship is going from strength to strength.

Optimism is the motivator that is essential for success, and it lies at the core of the positive psychology approach to resilience and recovering your wellbeing.

7. Value Relationships

Q: What do the happiest people have in common?

A: They are highly social and have close relationships.

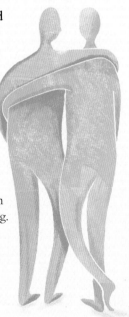

No man, or woman, is an island. We all have a need to connect and belong. This is one of three fundamental needs for wellbeing, along with a sense of autonomy and competence.

Love is about connection, and to love is one of the major ways to increase your happiness, raising both psychological and physical wellbeing. The absence of connection breeds loneliness, which can trigger mental-health issues.

Love is...connection

Fortunately the benefits of love are not the preserve of couples and family relationships. In *Love 2.0*, Professor Barbara Fredrickson defines love as a micro-moment of warmth and connection shared with another living being. It can even happen with a stranger. Three things occur in a moment of "positivity resonance": a shared experience of positive emotions, the syncing of behaviour and biochemistry, and a mutual impulse to care for each other.

Love lab

One key finding from the "Love Lab" set up by Professor Emeritus John Gottman at the University of Washington is the existence of a "positivity ratio". For a relationship to flourish, it requires a ratio of 5:1 – five positive emotional events for every one negative experience. To put it another way, it takes five positives to repair the damage of one negative event. This really highlights how negativity has the potential to harm a relationship.

How to communicate

The way we interact can help or hinder a relationship. Defensiveness, stonewalling, criticism and contempt all negatively impact upon a relationship. Professor Shelly Gable at the University of California has identified four communication styles, which are revealed by how we respond to someone's good news, as shown below.

WAYS OF RESPONDING

PASSIVE DESTRUCTIVE

Ignores the news, changes the focus

"Listen to what happened to me."

PASSIVE CONSTRUCTIVE

Quiet, low-energy support

"I suppose that's nice."

ACTIVE DESTRUCTIVE

Quashes the event

"That sounds stressful."

ACTIVE CONSTRUCTIVE

Enthusiastic, energetic support

"That's great! Tell me more…"

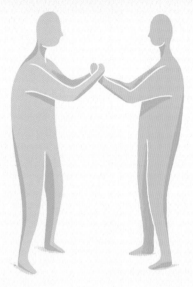

After looking at the chart on page 69, you may already have guessed that active-constructive responding (ACR) is a way of responding to someone's good news with energy, enthusiasm and excitement and is the only style that supports relationships. Ideally, you would then follow up with questions, so that the person with good news can capitalize on the positive emotions that it generates. It may surprise you to learn that it is more important to nurture the relationship by practising ACR in good times than it is to provide a shoulder to cry on during bad times.

ACTIVITY:

Loving-kindness Meditation

This Buddhist meditation, known as *metta bhavana*, opens the heart to be warm and loving toward others by wishing them health and happiness. It produces such a range of positive emotions that it can outpace hedonic adaptation (see page 29), whereby we take our happiness for granted.

1 Sit comfortably, taking a few deep breaths to relax the body. Focus on the heart, by hovering a hand over it.

2 Direct loving kindness toward yourself by repeating the following: *"May I be happy. May I be well. May I be safe. May I be peaceful and at ease."*

3 Then extend your focus outward, in turn, to people you love, your acquaintances, those you're estranged from and the wider world. *"May you be happy. May you be well. May you be safe. May you be peaceful and at ease."*

4 Savour the feeling of warmth as it grows.

8. Practise Kindness

Kindness is the virtue of doing good deeds for others without any expectation of personal gain. With a splash of empathy, compassion, generosity, care, altruism and love, you have some of the many faces of kindness.

Acts of kindness are a win–win. They are good for you and for the greater good. Kindness feeds happiness, oils the wheels of relationships and creates positive communities. It puts the "kind" into "kindred spirit" and is the very essence of humanity. Volunteers often experience a "helpers' high", which can be a distraction from their own troubles and an antidote to low mood.

Kindness and gratitude are a double act and you can count kindnesses in a similar way to recording good things in a gratitude journal (see page 46). When acts of kindness are met with gratitude, the positive emotions bounce back and forth between the giver and recipient, strengthening the relationship. Even witnessing a kind act is elevating and, because positive emotions are contagious, one kind act can inspire another and set off a chain reaction, which you see in "random acts of kindness" and "pay it forward" projects.

Avoiding compassion fatigue

When it comes to kindness, it's worth remembering the oxygen-mask principle: look after yourself before attending to others. Compassion fatigue can set in if your own needs are ignored. Self-compassion means treating yourself with kindness, and self-care is a prerequisite for your own happiness.

Practising kindness

There is a strong connection between performing kindnesses for others and your own personal level of happiness, but to gain the benefits, your good deeds need to be motivated by selfless – rather than selfish – reasons.

It doesn't matter what you do; a small, local kindness can work as well as a grand gesture. Your acts of kindness may be spontaneous or planned, but research suggests that concentrating them in a single day will deliver a greater boost to your happiness than spreading them out.

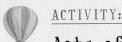

ACTIVITY:

Acts of Kindness

Here are some ideas to get you started, or to add variety to what you already do. Notice how you feel immediately after performing a good deed.

- Pay for someone's coffee, parking or travel.

- Befriend a neighbour and lend them a helping hand.

- Volunteer with a local charity or surprise someone with the gift of your time.

- Buy a homeless person a night in a hostel.

- Be considerate: open the door for someone, carry a heavy bag, let someone go ahead of you in a line.

- Invite someone over to share a meal.

- Pay someone a compliment; tell them what you appreciate about them.

- Talk to someone who is on their own at a social event.

9. Get Physical

You've probably heard of "psychosomatic" illnesses – how the mind influences the body in a negative way. But what about "somatopsychic" wellbeing, where the body influences the mind in a positive way?

Using the body–mind connection is much underrated as a means of growing your happiness. Even the simple act of breathing deeply can change your state, putting the brakes on stress and restoring calm.

Exercise as a mood-booster

Physical activity is a natural antidepressant. A study carried out at Duke University School of Medicine in North Carolina compared three groups with major depression. One group was treated with antidepressant pills, another did exercise and a third had a combination of both. All three groups recovered, but ten months down the line the group with the lowest relapse rate was the exercisers.

Physical contact can also boost our mood. A hug reduces stress levels and increases oxytocin, the "love hormone". Massage and other physical therapies activate the parasympathetic nervous system, which puts the body into a state of relaxation. The joy of sex is that not only does it feel good, but it also calms the mind, increases trust and deepens the bonds of the couple.

Positive Psychology in Motion

I often recommend physical activity to clients, for a quick and easy mood lift. Moving the body releases endorphins, which trigger a positive feeling in the mind. Anything that raises the heart rate will release these hormones. Follow these tips and get moving.

- Aim for 30 minutes of moderate exercise five days a week. This can be divided into shorter bursts, such as two 15-minute walks around the park.

- Choose an activity that you are drawn to, such as Argentinian tango, skateboarding, gardening or wild swimming, to stay motivated.

- Make it social: find an exercise buddy or join a sports team.

- Build exercise into your daily routine. Take the stairs rather than the lift. Get off the bus one stop early.

- Use an app to keep count of how many steps you do each day.

- Rate your mood out of ten before and after physical activity.

- Exercise in nature for an even bigger mood boost (see page 83).

You are what you eat

Food affects mood – negatively, in the case of sugar. Sweet snacks and comfort foods can bring you down after the initial sugar high. But you can also eat and drink your way to greater wellbeing, as these two key examples show.

 Water is essential not only for survival, but also for wellbeing. A glass of water can perk you up. For optimal functioning, the brain needs enough hydration to bring energy in and send signals out to the rest of the body. A lack of hydration is linked to low mood and depression.

Serotonin is the brain chemical known as the "happy hormone", which induces restful sleep and promotes wellbeing. Low serotonin levels are linked to depression and anxiety. Eating proteins such as meat, fish, beans and eggs helps to make tryptophan, the amino acid that is needed to produce serotonin.

Healthy mind, healthy body

Homeostasis is a state of equilibrium where the body's systems are in balance – and the same applies for a healthy mind. We need rest and adequate sleep to balance the busyness of modern life. The mistake is to ignore the body and keep going until you crash. Whereas stress has a negative impact on the body, research is now showing that happiness has the opposite effect – a protective influence on the same biological pathways. It's a case of psychosomatic wellness: the mind affecting the body in a positive way.

10. Turn to Nature

Just as the physical body can act as a channel to greater wellbeing, so does the natural environment. Nature is a great healer, reducing stress, lifting the mood and helping you to health and happiness.

Immersion in fresh air and foliage provides an instant digital detox, counteracting the mental fatigue of an over-stimulated mind. Your brain functions better in nature, which improves concentration and cognitive ability, as well as boosting wellbeing. Simply looking at images of nature is calming and is linked to higher levels of alpha brainwave activity, which plays a role in serotonin production (see page 81).

Green and blue

"Green exercise" means doing physical activity such
as running, cycling, horseriding or sailing in a natural
environment. If you're wired and tired, the idea of heading
to the gym may be too much to contemplate, but it only
takes five minutes of physical activity in a green space to start
generating positive emotions. Engaging in green exercise
by water – aka a "blue environment" – such as the sea, lakes
or rivers, produces the greatest improvement in mood.

Cultivating happiness

"Ecotherapy" harnesses the power of nature to help people recover their wellbeing. Treatment can take the form of any outdoor activity and is often done with other people – for example, volunteering in a community garden or farm, looking after animals, conservation work, fruit picking, and arts and crafts in nature.

Gardening is a prime example of ecotherapy. Not only is it a mood-booster, but growing food can also provide a sense of purpose to anyone lacking motivation. There's an added bonus to getting your hands into the earth. Soil contains a common microbe called *Mycobacterium vaccae*, which has an effect on brain neurons that resembles antidepressants. Getting dirty can make you happy!

ACTIVITY:

Forest Bathing

There's something deeply refreshing about being out in the woods. The Japanese have elevated time spent among trees into a healing therapy known as *shinrin-yoku*, which means bathing in the forest.

Immersion in a natural environment activates the body's parasympathetic nervous system (see page 77), lowering stress hormones, replenishing energy stores and building vitality. Just 20 minutes is enough to induce a state of calm. (Don't have access to a forest? Practise this in any open green space.)

1 Stand in one spot and open yourself up to the forest through the senses.

2 Look around. What can you see?

3 Pick up twigs, leaves or stones and feel their texture.

4 What can you hear? Notice birdsong, wind in the trees or the rustling of leaves.

5 Breathe. Feel the air in your lungs and on your skin.

6 Note the smells of nature around you.

11. Practise Mindfulness

"Mindfulness" is about developing awareness – of the thoughts, feelings and bodily sensations going on inside us, and of the world around us.

With a multiplicity of demands in modern life, the average attention span is shorter than ever. "Mindlessness" describes how we end up going through the motions without taking anything in – such as eating something without tasting it.

Mindfulness meditation brings us into the present moment, reminding us that we are human "beings" rather than human "doings". It's easy to miss out on the joys of the here-and-now when we're brooding over the past or getting worked up about the future. Mindfulness helps us recognize that thoughts and emotions are like the weather – they come and go – so that we are less likely to be triggered by them.

Mindfulness and happiness

Professor Richard Davidson, a neuroscientist at the University of Wisconsin, has found that the eight-week course in Mindfulness-based Stress Reduction (MBSR) develops the left prefrontal cortex, the left side of the brain's frontal lobe, which is where positive emotions are activated. So regular practice of mindfulness meditation can help increase your capacity for happiness. It certainly worked for me. I felt as if I'd been subtly rewired for happiness.

And that isn't the only way mindfulness – a Buddhist practice with benefits for mental health – can help. People strive to fulfil their desires, such as the longing for happiness, which can cause them to suffer when it proves elusive. Buddhists encourage acceptance and non-attachment, which involves letting go of striving, so that we are free of the cycle of craving and disappointment.

Mindfulness also leads to "kindfulness": a mindful compassion in the way we handle ourselves and relate to others.

Being mindful every day

The simplest way to practise mindfulness is to sit in a relaxed position and focus on your breath coming in and going out. It is entirely normal for the mind to wander, so gently bring your attention back to the breath whenever it does so.

The senses are also a good way into mindfulness, even via something as mundane as an everyday chore. Try doing the washing up by hand. Notice the sensation of hot and cold water on your hands, the sound of water running, the fragrance of dishwashing liquid and the welcome sight of the plates coming up sparkly clean. You could even snack on a tasty morsel from a plate, to cover all five senses!

Being mindful also supports the other Happiness Habits – for example, it can enhance the connection to nature.

ACTIVITY:

The Three-step Breathing Space

When you find your mood spiralling in a negative direction, this short mindfulness meditation can bring you back into the present moment and help you to access inner peace. Allow around a minute for each step.

1 Become aware of what's going on right now in your mind, body and around you. Acknowledge it and let it be.

2 Focus on a single point of the breath in the body, such as in the belly. Notice all the sensations.

3 Now expand your awareness to include your whole body and any other sensations that may be present.

MINDFULNESS

focus on the present

Deliberate, non-judgemental attention to what is happening in the present moment

FLOW

focus on the activity

Total immersion in what you're doing, with a loss of self-consciousness

SAVOURING

focus on the positive

Focus on positive experiences in past, present or future

Mindfulness, savouring and flow

If you think mindfulness sounds a bit like "savouring" or "flow" (see pages 48 and 18), you're right. These Happiness Habits *are* related, but whereas mindfulness is about focusing on the present without judgement, there is an intention behind savouring, which is to cultivate positive emotion; and flow is about being fully absorbed in the activity.

12. Strive for Success

Our final Happiness Habit, and the remaining ingredient in the PERMA model of wellbeing (see page 16), is A for Accomplishment – or striving for success.

People are motivated to achieve: the sweet taste of triumph makes us feel good. It might be about beating the competition to win the prizes, but equally it could be about your own personal development and making progress along your chosen path.

Happiness and success are universal desires and there is a strong relationship between them. Experiencing success leads to happiness, but the reverse is also true, and people with high levels of wellbeing tend to enjoy more success. When you're happy, you are most likely to be engaged and productive.

ACTIVITY:

Frame Your Intention

Not all goals are created equal, so to maximize your chances of success and raise your wellbeing, it helps to frame your intention as:

🐦 **A goal that you want to move toward (*approach*) rather than something you want to escape from (*avoid*).** For instance, relocating to somewhere rural because you want the fresh air (*approach*), rather than escaping the town because of the pollution (*avoid*). Avoidance goals are stressful because you've constantly got your eye on the negatives. Approach goals, on the other hand, lead to the presence of something positive.

🐦 **Something you are intrinsically motivated to do.** An *intrinsic* goal is one you want to accomplish for its own sake because it's inherently interesting or enjoyable. An *extrinsic* goal is usually motivated by an external reward, such as money, or is done to impress. It often reflects something that other people approve of or want for us, rather than our own deep desire. Focusing on extrinsic goals has a negative association with wellbeing.

🐔 **A goal that will give you the opportunity to satisfy the three fundamental needs for wellbeing.** Having a sense of *autonomy*, *competence* and *relatedness* in the task are the three essentials that will keep your motivation up, according to Professors Edward Deci and Richard Ryan who developed Self-Determination Theory (SDT). These are the psychological nutrients that can support your personal growth.

🐔 **A chance to use your strengths** (see page 51). These inner resources can be leveraged to help you achieve your goal. They are also a source of energy to make it happen. When you apply your strengths to a meaningful goal, the door opens to eudaimonic wellbeing (see page 10).

A Final Word

Psychology has traditionally focused on exploring our past in order to fix the present, but now the lens is turning toward the way we think about the future and how that shapes our wellbeing. The key to our happiness, according to Professor Martin Seligman, may lie in "prospection", our unique ability to contemplate the future. A final habit to get into, therefore, is that of visualizing a positive future.

Your "best possible self" is a journalling practice that involves writing about how you would like your life to be when everything has worked out for the best. Take a moment to imagine your life at a point in the future. What is the best possible life you can think of? Consider all areas of your life, such as career, relationships, interests and health. Doing this practice for 15 minutes a day has benefits for psychological and physical health and sparks the motivation to make the vision a reality.

Wishing you well in creating your happy future,

Miriam
www.positivepsychologytraining.co.uk

References

All websites accessed January 2019.

Introduction

Page 7: N L Sin and S Lyubomirsky, "Enhancing well-being and alleviating depressive symptoms with positive psychology interventions: A practice-friendly meta-analysis", *Journal of Clinical Psychology* (2009), 65, 467–87

1. What is Happiness?

Page 14: E Diener, "Subjective well-being: The science of happiness and a proposal for a national index", *American Psychologist* (2000), 55(1), 34–43

Page 15: Martin Seligman, *Authentic Happiness* (2002), Nicholas Brealey Publishing

Page 16: Martin Seligman, *Flourish* (2011), Nicholas Brealey Publishing

Page 18: Mihaly Csikszentmihalyi, *Flow* (2002), Rider

2. The Benefits of Happiness

Page 23: D Danner, D Snowdon and W Friesen, "Positive emotions in early life and longevity: Findings from the nun study", *Journal of Personality and Social Psychology* (2001), 80, 804–13

Page 25: Barbara Fredrickson, *Positivity* (2009), Crown Publishers

3. The Barriers to Happiness

Page 32: Barry Schwartz, *The Paradox of Choice* (2005), Harper Perennial

4. Happiness is a Practice

Page 38: Carol S Dweck, *Mindset* (2006), Constable & Robinson

5. The 12 Happiness Habits

Page 43: www.reading-well.org.uk/books/books-on-prescription

Page 44: Michael B Frisch, *Quality of Life Therapy* (2005), Wiley

Page 46: Sonja Lyubomirsky, *The How of Happiness* (2007), Sphere Books

Page 48: Fred B Bryant and Joseph Veroff, *Savoring: A New Model of Positive Experience* (2007), Lawrence Erlbaum Associates

Page 53: A Linley, *Average to A+* (2008), CAPP Press

Page 56: S Oishi and E Diener, "Residents of poor nations have a greater sense of meaning in life than residents of wealthy nations", *Psychological Science* (2014), 25, 422–30

Page 63: Martin Seligman, *Learned Optimism* (1998), Pocket Books

Page 68: Barbara L Fredrickson, *Love 2.0* (2013), Hudson Street Press

Page 68: www.gottman.com/love-lab/

Page 69: S Gable, H Reis, E Impett and E Asher, "What Do You Do When Things Go Right? The Intrapersonal and Interpersonal Benefits of Sharing Positive Events", *Journal of Personality and Social Psychology* (2004), 87(2), 228–45

Page 77: M Babyak, J Blumenthal *et al.*, "Exercise treatment for major depression: Maintenance of therapeutic benefit at 10 months", *Psychosomatic Medicine* (2000), 62, 633–8

Page 87: R J Davidson, J Kabat-Zinn, *et al.*, "Alterations in brain and immune function produced by mindfulness meditation" *Psychosomatic Medicine* (2003), 65(4), 564–70

Page 93: www.selfdeterminationtheory.org

Page 94: Martin Seligman, Peter Railton, Roy Baumeister, Chandra Sripada, *Homo Prospectus* (2016), OUP USA